CODSALL VILLAGE HISTORY TRAIL

A production by:

Codsall & Bilbrook History Society

Bramblewood Publishing
3 Bramblewood Close,
Overton-on-Dee, North Wales, LL13 0HJ
Email: Bramblewoodpublishing@outlook.com

© Donald V Walls and Codsall & Bilbrook History Society, 2025

Codsall & Bilbrook History Society is a registered charity: 503843.
For more information on the Society, visit codsallhistory.org

All rights reserved. No part of this publication may be reproduced or transmitted in any form or by any means, electronic or mechanical, including photocopying, recording or any information storage or retrieval system, without prior permission from the publishers.

First Edition published 2009 by Codsall & Bilbrook History Society.
Second, revised edition published by Bramblewood Publishing, 2025.
This impression: February 4th, 2026

ISBN: 978-0-9954996-4-5

Cover design: Robert J Davies
The cover photograph was originally black and white and has been colourised.
Designed and typeset in 11pt Times New Roman by Robert J Davies
Printed and bound in Great Britain

CODSALL VILLAGE HISTORY TRAIL

DV Walls

BRAMBLEWOOD
PUBLISHING

INTRODUCTION

DONALD WALLS was not born in Codsall but came here at the age of two in 1932. He lived in the village all his early life, going to the small school on top of the hill behind the church. He passed the scholarship exam at 11 to go to Brewood Grammar School where he stayed until he was 18 and then had to do his national service. On completion of this, he went to Harper Adams College to study Agriculture.

Donald V Walls

Afterwards Don went to work as the Farm Manager on a large estate in Shropshire. Then came the opportunity he really wanted which was to go to Africa on a two-year contract. Just when he and Mima his wife were due to come home, he was offered a contract in Southern Rhodesia. He took it but five years later in 1965, Rhodesian Prime Minister Ian Smith declared UDI and everything changed. Don came back to England the following year to once again make his home in Codsall, in Fairfield Drive where the family remained to the present day.

Not long after his return to the village, the vicar, Revd Gilbert Smith, invited Don to join the Parochial Church Council (PCC). He was to remain on it for 41 years without a break. During that time, he was church warden for 14 years and became chairman of the Churchyard Committee, something which was particularly close to his heart. At the same time he served for 15 years on the Parish Council and was chairman of the school governors of St Nicholas School.

During the last two years I have enjoyed accompanying Don – now a sprightly 95 – on walks around the village. His memory of

Codsall dating back to between the wars is remarkable and needs to be recorded and passed on. The bracketed numbers in bold in the text correspond with those on the diagrammatic plan to be found on the back of this booklet.

For readers interested in the historical background to these buildings, please refer to the Appendix at the back of the book which will give you more information. The Appendix, which follows the same numbers as in the main text, was originally produced for the Society by John Blamire-Brown and David Whitehead in 1998. It has long been out of print so it is very pleasing to be able to republish it in this new booklet which we very much hope you will enjoy and find useful.

Judy Davies
Chairman,
Codsall & Bilbrook History Society,
December 2025.

The walk with Don begins at Codsall Village Hall . . .

THE VILLAGE Hall was opened in 1964. The fields stretched from here right up to St Nicholas Church **(37)**. There were a lot of damson trees in the hedges and in the Spring it was a magnificent sight to see the white blossom stretching up the hillside.

On the opposite side of the road was The Wheel Pub, believed to have been built in 1848 when the railway came into the village. The licence was transferred to The Wheel from The Bush when the Old Vicarage was built.

The Bentley family kept the pub in the early 1900s. They were connected to the Wilkes family who owned a lot of land in Codsall. At the back of The Wheel were cottages before the housing estate was developed in the mid-1950s. Sadly, the pub was demolished in 2005.

The Wheel pub as it looked in 1910.

On the other side of the road was a walkway going between houses to the right – this was once the track which led to Vaughan Buildings which are still there **(24)**. The track was wide enough to take a vehicle and was an entrance to Roseville Dairy Farm rickyard, owned by Mr Lee (*see page 10*). There was a footpath over the field. We kept to the path when we went along it, because at school we were told that Mr Warner had kindly given permission for it to be used but we should not stray off it.

Another track, nearer the village, goes from the Wolverhampton Road between two fence panels. This walkway now takes you through to the Coronation Tree in Walton Gardens. The road was named after Mrs Walton who lived there. The tree was planted in 1937 to commemorate the Coronation of George VI.

At the top of Walton Gardens there is a lovely leafy footpath which goes up to Drury Lane. Where it meets the lane, there used to be a stile leading into Warner's Field. Fruit trees, including Tettenhall Dick, grew on the right-hand side. The Tettenhall Dick produced very small, yellow pears. They didn't keep very well, but like damsons were a feature of the area.

Warner's Field was used for Silver Jubilee celebrations for George V in 1935 and the Coronation celebrations for the new king two years later. There were several magnificent specimen sweet chestnut trees and several fruit trees in the field including more Tettenhall Dick. The field was also used for the annual event to crown the May Queen. Children from St Nicholas School danced around the maypole, having rehearsed these dances in the playground for weeks before the 'Big Day'.

At the junction with Drury Lane there used to be three cottages, joined together opening straight onto the lane. In one of them lived a road repairman. In those days when a repair was needed they took a boiler to the site. The boiler was fired to melt the tar and when the tar was in place they would cool it down with water from a watering can and then a steam roller would roll over the patches. Looking to the right would have been Warner's Field.

It stretched right over to Sandy Lane and as far as the orchards and gardens of the smallholdings and large houses in Elliotts Lane. St Nicholas School was built on Warner's Field. Farmer

Lee, who owned the farmhouse situated on the small island on the bypass, used to graze his milk cows on the land. He also used the field on the other side of Wolverhampton Road which possibly belonged to Mr Wilkes.

Back in Walton Gardens, a footpath went towards the Wolverhampton Road and another off to the left running along a wooden fence. It was overgrown so was difficult to walk along, but it still exists and comes out at the back of Vaughan Buildings then continues along the side of the buildings to finish at their front.

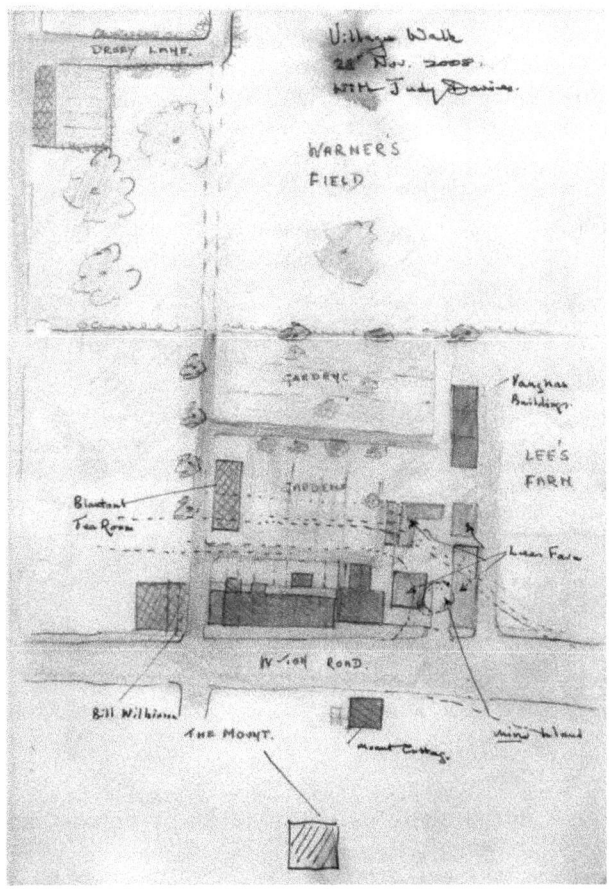

Don's sketch map showing the site of the former Lee's Farm between Warner's Field and the Wolverhampton Road.

If you stand near the roundabout on the Wolverhampton Road and look at the white arrow on the road, that is where the old farmhouse stood with its farm buildings at the back. They were all demolished to make way for the new bypass. **(23)**

The farmhouse was built quite close to the cottages. The grass that you see on the side of the cottages could well have been where the front lawn of Lee's Farm finished, with a little wall and a path leading up to the front door. In the area landscaped for The Lone Singer **(44)** there is a large stone block with a ring in it. This came from Lee's farm. Mr Lee used to buy in cattle to fatten up and sell on. They used to arrive on a train at the cattle pens in Chapel Lane. He would meet the train and walk them through the village to his farm. He used to rent the fields down at Gunstone where they would be grown on until big enough to be brought back and put on the train to be sent on.

Roseville Dairy in 1935, owned by Farmer Lee.

Farmer Lee and his wife had three children, two sons and a daughter. When the daughter was a teenager she went with her two older brothers and their girlfriends to a Saturday night party using the parents' car. In those days there were very few cars on the roads. On the return journey, the driver lost control, they crashed and she died in the wreckage. Such a tragedy rocked Codsall.

During the war years, all private cars were taken off the road and only people in essential occupations such as the doctor and the vicar were allowed to buy petrol and drive a car. Road accidents were extremely rare. Eileen Gilks, a long-time resident of Codsall, can only remember one traffic accident when she was a child. It happened on a Sunday lunchtime at the crossroads of Station Road and Wood Road. The Codsall policeman was called to the scene. He walked casually from the police station **(8)** behind the War Memorial **(7)** to the accident. When he got there he realised he had forgotten his notebook and pencil, so he had to walk back to collect them! Meantime, the individuals involved in the collision had to wait patiently for him to come back.

The cottages here on the right as you approach the village all had large, long gardens and at the end, each one had a washhouse and pigsty. The washhouses had copper boilers and on Monday mornings, you would see smoke coming out of the chimneys. The owners also kept hens. At the back, between the cottages and their gardens, was a communal walkway. The walkway had outbuildings which served as the communal toilet and their washhouses. The same families lived in the cottages for years. On the other side of the main road is a cul-de-sac called Mount Gardens. This was the main entrance into what was a large Victorian House called The Mount. **(17)** It was the home of the Loveridge family until it was demolished in 1968.

The Mount: built in 1840, knocked down in 1968.

The Mount, built in 1840, had extensive, beautifully landscaped gardens which stretched from the Wheel Field in one direction to the grounds of The Bull in the other. The Loveridges built Mount Cottage **(21)** for Mr and Mrs Medlicott who worked for them in their house and garden. They left it to Mrs Medlicott.

Number 6A was where the Home Guard used to meet, before they moved over to the other side of the road to the building which had the siren on its roof, **(20)** which went off to warn people of imminent air-raids and to signal the All Clear. This was also the site of an old barnyard. Later, there was a public toilet built on the Wheel Field. Like many others it was misused and had to be closed.

The cottages fronting the pavement into the village formed part of the main built-up area of Codsall. Cottage no. 29 was Stevenson's Fish & Chip shop. Cottage no. 23 was a butcher's belonging to Mr Harper. The two metal supports which held the sign can still be seen in the wall. Where the launderette is now was Freddy Blanton's very good General Store and of course Blanton's Tea Room **(22)** at the back belonged to him. At the side of the store was the walkway to the tearoom which was situated just about where the bollards are between the two parking areas adjacent to the ring-road.

Blanton's Tea Room was the largest meeting place in the village, so it was the venue for many activities. Eric Reed's mother bought the building for the Forget-Me-Not-Club, partly with a grant from the George VI Memorial Fund and partly with money she had raised. Eric's father was the Treasurer until he became ill. At that point Mrs Ray took over and ran it until the building was burnt down in 1968. She did the catering there, ran jumble sales for charities and took coal round to people who needed it.

When we had big events, like the 1935 Silver Jubilee and the 1937 Coronation on Warner's Field – at the end, we would go straight down to Blanton's Tea Room or pop and buns and on those occasions we were presented with a commemorative mug. On the other side of the walkway was a cobbler's shop belonging to Stan Wake and then Bill Wilkinson. Joining onto this was a tall building occupied by Beardmore and Lowe, painters and decorators. This was once the site of the tiny Primitive Methodist Chapel, used until the Methodist Chapel was built in Chapel Lane.

Blanton's Tea Room on fire in 1968. The end of an era.

Then there were two wooden-framed shops with their frontages onto what is today's pavement. The first shop was a draper's shop belonging to Mrs Rhona Jenkins. *(See photo overleaf.)* The second was Mr White's greengrocery shop.

Next was the half-timbered house **(19)** *(see overleaf)* where Mr Latham lived. At one time it had a front garden with a stone wall separating the garden from the pavement. It is possibly the oldest building in Codsall. For many years it was a restaurant called Franco's. Today, it is awaiting new tenants.

On the corner now occupied by the Building Society, was Harvey's Post Office and General Store. **(18)** Mr Harvey had his finger on the pulse of the village, besides being the postmaster he owned the blacksmith's and the wheelwright's, where coffins were made for funerals and repairs carried out.

Top: Jenkins' shop and left: the half-timbered building reputed to be the oldest in Codsall.

In the brick wall on the side of the Building Society there is a small area of new brick filling in the gap left when the postbox was removed. Later the Postmaster was called 'Lockie Law', because of his involvement with coffins. He delivered telegrams in wartime which always heralded bad news.

Harvey's store in Codsall Square before the War.

Round the corner were two shops where Love & Liquor is now. The first was Bannister & Thatcher's, the chemist. The building also housed Foyles Library. The second was occupied by Mr Screen, the barber. What was the chemist's shop until recently is in a new building on land which would have been part of the substantial gardens belonging to the houses.

The Bull pub on the other side of the road had a wall around the front as well as round the Bowling Green at the back. There was a magnificent line of elm trees along the wall at the end of The Bull's gardens. These succumbed to Dutch Elm disease in the late 1960s. The front wall of The Bull was demolished when the road had to be widened to accommodate the buses when a service to Wolverhampton began in 1923. *(See photo overleaf.)*

In the middle of the landscaped garden is a statue called The Lone

The Bull pub in the Square.

Singer, **(44)** the work of Sir Charles Wheeler who lived in the black and white house to be seen on the left-hand side of Church Road on the other side of Baker's Way bypass. The road up to St Nicholas Church **(37)** started here, passing on the right-hand side, a lovely Georgian building which housed the Printing Press. **(25)**

This Georgian building housed the Printing Press.

It was demolished for the bypass. It lay back about 15 yards from the pavement, starting about where the telegraph pole is, it ran parallel with the road. Mr Denton was the printer. Village people were able to register Births and Deaths at the Cottage Press one day each week. Before that they went to the house where the Jones family lived further up Church Road.

On the end of the Printing Press was a little cottage with a sloping roof, where Mrs Walton lived and her son Jack. Her garden met Mrs Rowland's garden from her cottages near the half-timbered house. Her aunt, Mrs Prince, had a little sweetshop that used to come right onto the road. At this time, until it closed, there were two sweetshops in Church Road.

On the left-hand side of the road with its door opening on to Bakers Way is Russell House, **(43)** now a private residence, but once called Baker's House when it was the house for the hugely important Bakers Nursery. The main entrance into the Nursery is now the back entrance to Russell House. Immediately opposite were the buildings housing the smithy and wheelwright **(26)**.

The Smithy in 1935.

On the right of them was an old building, not used very much, then the wheelwright and smithy on the end. Mr Cooper made the coffins. He was Mrs Rowland's brother.

Almost everybody was related to someone else in the village. Bill Pascal was the blacksmith when Bill Booth joined him in about 1940. From here up to the entrance to Warner's Field was a wall about four feet high. On the opposite side and still there is the black and white house known as Wheeler's House after the sculptor Sir Charles Wheeler, who was born there.

Birthplace of Sir Charles Wheeler.

The house was also the site of the first village Post Office. This occupied a tin hut on the left-hand side. Mrs Cumberland lived in the house at one time. She was joined by Miss Loveridge when The Mount was demolished. Then the actress Mrs Harnetty went to live there. Her stage name was Penelope Shaw. Her brother, Sebastian Shaw, was in Return of the Jedi.

A little higher up and opposite the entrance to Warner's Field was Warner's house *(see photo opposite)*. It was a substantial Georgian-style dwelling lying back from the road behind a stone wall, now demolished. Between there and the Parish Rooms **(41)** were gardens.

If you went along a path towards the back of the Parish Rooms there was a little cobbler's shop where Mr Jones, brother of Mrs Cockerill, mended shoes. The buildings next door are two substantial houses going right up to the corner of Church Lane,

Warner's house, opposite the entrance to Warner's Field.

which belonged to the Jones family. Mr and Mrs Jones lived in the first house with two daughters. Three other sisters lived next door. One of them was a physiotherapist at the Royal Hospital and she made FMS ointment. Mrs Cockerill, (a Jones before she married) always had it at school and would rub it on the children's grazes. It was supposed to be very good for leg ulcers and people would go to the house to buy it.

At the back of No. 26 was a well with the date on it in the 1700s. It was capped in 2006. Back on the right-hand side, the road widened into a semi-circle which marked the entrance into Warner's Field. The first part was a garden and then the field which was the venue for the school's Sports Day and other special village events, particularly May Day celebrations.

At the end of Warner's Field on Church Road were a row of cottages. In the first one was the sweet shop *(see photo overleaf)* frequented by the children on their way up to school. Several people ran the shop, but most people remember Mrs Fenn – the last person to keep it. In the last house lived a very thin man nicknamed Fat Harry. Then came Drury Lane. The other side of it was a house with a big wooden gate and at the back was a wooden building which was the Working Men's Club **(29)**. It was also the Post Office sorting office. Opposite, in what is a garage today, there was a door in the wall and this was Albert Hughes' wet fish shop. Albert used a pony and trap to take the fish around the village. He was also the local gravedigger.

The little sweet shop in Church Road.

On the corner where Drury Lane comes out onto Church Road was a Working Men's Club and then cottages all the way up the road. Just before the white building, which is near the top today, was the Co-op. *(See photo opposite)*. Turning into Church Lane you pass a stone in the wall of Manor Court **(40)** with three dates inscribed on it: 1784, 1857 and 1983. Originally the house was called Clifton House.

Continuing up Church Lane, just before the churchyard, is a footpath which goes all the way to Chillington Lane. This was the route used by the Codsall Wood children who walked to the school behind the Church. The school playing fields were at the back of the churchyard. There are two cottages next door. Mr Jebb, a waggoner at Bakers Nursery, lived in one of them.

Back on the right-hand side were pebble-dashed cottages. The top cottage No. 53 had stable doors and was once a butcher's shop. The Illidge family lived there. Stan Illidge was a bellringer. Joe Illidge, his brother, was killed in the Second World War. Mr Illidge was a postman. Next door to them was the original Co-operative shop, **(30)** before it moved down into Station Road. It was a strange building for a shop, with very high windows and high ceilings inside. Was it built as a Co-op or had it been something else before? Everything seemed very new. There were big, smart bacon slicers. A few school-leavers went to work there when they left school. The cottages have been replaced by bungalows. The other side of the Co-op was a cottage with a thatched roof, replaced with a new house built for Mrs Smith and her son.

The original Co-op shop in Church Road.

The top of Church Road with the Co-op in the distance.

Number 46 on the left-hand side was the position of the off-licence. It was looked after by Mr Ward until it was taken over later by Mrs Green when she left the Cross Guns at Codsall Wood. The new dwelling next door was built in what was formerly the Vicarage vegetable garden.

Behind the Church was the school **(34)** where all local children went until the 11+. After the age of eleven they either stayed there or went on to Brewood Grammar, Wolverhampton Grammar / High etc., until the new Secondary School opened in 1940. At the back of the school was the Mill House **(35)** – once the local windmill many years ago. Going past the letterbox in the wall opposite the Church and turning into Sandy Lane, you soon come across the high wall of Brabourne House. **(31)**

This was the home of Mrs Miles Reece and her sister and was well known as the goat farm. This is on the corner of Drury Lane. There were three very humble cottages on the left in the lane. There have been finds in the area suggesting that this may have been an old graveyard. Located on the south side of the Church, it would certainly have been a favoured location.

The school attended by all pupils until they took the 11+. This is how it looked in 1952 from Mill Lane, with outside toilets down the middle of the playground, separating boys from girls. The bicycle sheds are on the right.

Return to the village centre . . .
Back down in the village on the right-hand side of The Crown Pub **(45)** were cottages. These were later demolished and when the buses came, a bus shelter was built there. In order to turn round and return to Wolverhampton, they had to back into Wood Road. Several times, the buses damaged the window of Stockton's shop. On Wednesdays and Saturdays the No. 15 went out to Codsall Wood, Bishops Wood and possibly out further to Blymhill, coming back again after about an hour.

Buses in those days did not have an ignition. They had to be cranked by the driver using considerable manual force to bring the engine to life. The engines were very noisy and the whole vehicle vibrated constantly in motion. As the Codsall bus rounded the corner into Church Road at the bus terminus, male passengers regularly jumped off the open rear platform rather than wait for the bus to stop. The upper deck was always fogged up by cigarette smoke. No smoking was allowed downstairs where the women and children travelled.

An open-topped omnibus outside The Crown in the Square.

All the buildings in the Codsall end of Wood Road belonged to Spencer's butcher's shop **(47)**. It had been in three generations of the Spencer family. They raised many of the animals themselves at Nursery Farm, their farm in Codsall Wood. The present-day hairdresser's shop was once part of Spencer's house with lovely tiles inside the front hall.

Old Mr and Mrs Spencer lived in the house. They both served in the shop and the slaughterhouse was next door at the back. It was a high-class butcher's. Old Frank Spencer was the epitome of an English farmer. He never actually seemed to do anything, but he was always there. Kate, his wife, used to sit on a stool behind a desk. When you paid she took your money and wrote it down.

Frank Spencer's butcher's shop as it looked in the 1930s.

It was the young couple, Harry and his wife, who did all the serving. They were a charming couple, always smartly dressed in white overalls. They lived in the white house in Chillington Lane where the cattle were raised. They had a proper wooden chopping block. On the floor was sawdust. Some of the meat was displayed but if anything else was required from the back, Walker – never

Mr Walker – would be summoned to bring it in. He was the slaughterman for the village and would go round and dispatch chickens and pigs for local people.

Spencer's wall went down to The Firs, which was originally a farmhouse. You now have to enter via the Co-op car park. During the War, the Firs outbuildings **(46)** were used as a factory with part-time ladies assembling and making small metal parts for aeroplanes. The ARP were also housed in the building.

The Square in Codsall in 1917, with The Bull on the left.

Going down Wood Road on the right-hand side, was a thatched cottage called Bank House where Mr and Mrs Barry lived. Mrs Barry made an ointment which they sold in Wolverhampton.

On the corner, now a solicitors and estate agent, was another general store **(48)**. Originally called York's Grocery and Provision Store it later became Stockton's. It was a large shop, occupying the whole of the corner premises, with display windows down the long side.

The sign on the door said that it was established in 1756. It catered for the more prosperous people in the community. Eric Reed was in charge of taking out the deliveries. Customers would phone up: number 117, place their order and he would take it out.

It was a very, very high-class grocery shop. When you ordered two or three things they were written down on a pad, in pencil of course, there were no biros in those days. Mr Stockton was a perfect English gentleman. He wore a smock over his collar and tie, but it was not an ordinary brown or white smock. It was a flecked, greyish-blue colour, and there was always a lovely welcoming smile as you went in.

The shop had the most delicious smells. There was freshly-sliced York ham and freshly-ground coffee. If you wanted tea, it was always loose tea and you chose from the range of varieties. It was then weighed out and Mr Stockton would put it into the middle of a piece of paper. He then proceeded to deftly fold the paper into a parcel which he tied up with a piece of string. There was a selection of papers for the different ingredients.

Everything you bought had to be weighed out, even pepper. You had to take your own bottles in for golden syrup and vinegar. The sugar was weighed out into blue bags. The butter came in big barrels and was cut up in the shop. The cheese was cut with a cheese wire. The bacon was hung up in flitches then sliced on the bacon slicer to whatever thickness you required.

Salt was often sold in large blocks, especially when people wanted a large quantity for curing the pig meat or salting down the beans. Eggs could be bought preserved in isinglass (a traditional gelatine preservative obtained from fish.)

Those days, before refrigerators, all the perishable goods were kept down in the cellar. Butter was only brought up into the shop in small quantities if the weather was warm. During and after the War it was very difficult to get greaseproof paper and it had to be cut into very small pieces to wrap around the butter. Of course, when food was rationed, the weekly rations for one person would fit into a tiny box, for example: one egg, an ounce of fat etc. If you needed several items it obviously took quite some time to do your shopping but people were used to queuing. The shop was open from 9am to 6pm every day except Wednesday as this was half-day closing, and Saturday when it stayed open until 7pm. Mr Stockton kept the shop from 1933 until he retired in 1963. Then the bank bought the premises and the shop closed.

Mr Stockton was second-in-command of the ATC Squadron in Codsall. On Friday night he opened up the rifle range in Wood Road. He had been in the Flying Corps in the First World War. Flight Lieutenant Stockton flew those planes made of wood and wire. He had an ancient Vauxhall car which he would start at high speed as though he was taking off in a plane. He would bring a couple of packets of Jacobs biscuits and a flagon of cider. We had an instructor who came and brought the rifles.

After we had shot our five rounds, we finished the evening with the crackers and cider. The rifle range was situated down Wood Road and was accessed from the road now called Oak Tree Rise. It was a brick-built building. Just before Oak Tree Rise were some steps which led into the club and then on your right was the bowling green. There were also the tennis courts up there.

During the War you had to register with a shop and they hadn't always got what you wanted so some weeks you would have to go without. Something like sugar for example and they would say, "We haven't got it this week, but we shall have it next week." You hoped they would have it and you would go on Monday morning and find fifty people waiting. Then there wasn't enough for everyone and you would have to go without again. It was a hard life.

A great many things were delivered to your door – coal, meat, bread, milk, vegetables and potatoes, which were bought by the hundredweight (cwt) and because they weren't washed, stored well and would last for months. Except for a few tinned items like pineapple and peaches, most things were fresh and you were only able to buy the things that were in season. Some apple varieties would last for months. Russets and Coxes were at their best at Christmas. Bramleys would last till March and there was always rhubarb in Codsall for most of the year, but you wouldn't expect to buy it in March.

Next, in Station Road, was a high tin fence with two big green gates in the middle which opened onto a yard in front of an open-fronted building. Round to the side of this building was one of the village wells. It is easy to see where a piece has been added onto the front of the old building. Mr Stockton used to keep his car in the yard during the daytime. At the back was a storeroom for the shop and a big open shed. From here were cottages fronting onto the pavement next to the road. In the second cottage Mr Law ran the Post Office after he moved the Post Office from the Square. At the side of these was a large white house.

Where the Forget-Me-Not rooms and the Co-op car park are now was the large business of Codsall Supply Company **(2)** owned by George Jones and his brother. They were well-known characters in the village. George lived at the bottom of Wood Road (possibly at no. 121 near the house that had the telephone exchange in the front room). George and his brother were involved in building the Methodist Chapel in Chapel Lane. George was superintendent of the Sunday School for some years.

At the front of the Supply Company were the office and shop. Behind these were the extensive sheds storing all the agricultural supplies for the local farmers. This was a large and busy organisation. Ann Reed's father, Joe Condlyffe, used to go to Liverpool docks in a large lorry to pick up grain and other supplies. He also did deliveries to local farmers.

I knew a lot about the Codsall Supply Company because I was very friendly with the sons of Mr Jones, the owner. We used to go and play on the hessian sacks at the back of the buildings. It was a very big concern selling everything the farmers around would need. All the foodstuffs came in hessian sacks and there were rats and mice everywhere. It was teeming with them! And in turn, the rodents were food for the numerous owls that lived nearby. How the people next door in Codsall House coped I did not know. Their land was immediately adjacent to the back of the Codsall Supply buildings.

The Forget-Me-Not building and the Parish Council building **(4)** were on land which had been part of Codsall House before it was bought by the Council. The Forget-Me-Not was built to replace Blanton's Tea Room, the wooden building situated behind the Dry Cleaners which, as noted before, burnt down in 1968. Over on the other side of the Square, next to The Bull **(16)**, was a row of shops and cottages which stretched from the end of The Bull wall around the corner into Wilkes Road.

A sandstone wall enclosed the end of their gardens with their washhouses and continued on to curl round at the back of The Bull to join the Wolverhampton Road. I remember how narrow the road was before the Second World War when the cottages on both sides of the road came almost to the edge of the highway, with only a small footpath in front of them. The first of the shops in this little row was Hancock's bicycle shop **(14)**.

Hancock's bicycle shop, in 1935.

As well as selling and repairing bikes it sold gun ammunition, recharged accumulators for people's radios and lots more besides. Mr Wall lived in the next cottage, then Mrs Wenlock. The living room of the cottage on the corner was a shop which sold homemade sweets. This was always called Granny Bird's, because Mrs Picken, who ran the shop, was a Bird before she got married. Her cat's favourite sleeping place was on top of the sweets in the window. On the other side of Wilkes Road were old, red sandstone storage barns for Codsall Supply Company.

House no. 29 in Station Road was known as Wellesley House and apart from the council houses it was the only one along the first part of the road. Granny Maybury, the village midwife, lived in the second council house from the War Memorial end. When she was old she was one of twelve people in the village to receive 'Church Bread' – a free loaf paid for out of one of the Church charities and given out each week. Maybury Close was named after her.

On the other side of Station Road was a gate at the entrance to Codsall House **(3)**. Fairfield Drive follows the entrance into Flemmynge House. **(5)** If you look carefully you can see that it cuts through lines of some old, attractive pine trees.

The Twentyman family on horseback at Flemmynge House.

Behind the War Memorial **(7)** was the building opened as the first Police Station **(6)**. The land belonged to the Codsall Charities. Mr Walker, Spencer's slaughterman, lived in one of the cottages. His mother could regularly be seen plucking fowl in the garden.

The road bridge for Codsall Station **(12)** was built in 1848 by the Shrewsbury and Birmingham Railway. The Station opened in 1849 and was mainly responsible for the growth of Codsall as a village of some importance. On the other side of the station entrance, where a building now stands back from the road, there used to be a Victorian shrubbery with a huge pampas grass as a feature. In the 1950s Mr Weston had a small kiosk there. Later that was demolished and replaced by Mr Heath's General Store.

On the corner across the road, there used to be a wooden building housing a general store. It also sold newspapers. Mrs Cook used to take the papers on her horse and trap. The local children would follow her around and she would give them the papers that needed delivering and they would run and put them through the doors for her.

She didn't pay them; they just did it for the fun of it. She lived in the farmhouse immediately behind her shop on the corner of Chapel Lane and The Broadway. The entrance was just in Chapel Lane through two large wooden doors. The farm buildings and stables ran alongside the pavement as far as the pebbledash houses. Mrs Cook's son Tom was a very good steeplechase jockey, even racing in the Grand National. After Mrs Cook gave up the shop it was run by Mr Weston who moved out of the kiosk. Then Angus Stewart occupied it until he moved into larger premises in the centre of Codsall, when it was taken over by Scraggs. Mrs Reeves had a crockery shop on the same corner. At one time, Mrs Paget did catering next to Cook's.

On the Station side of Chapel Lane **(9)** there were no houses. Lorries went up the main entrance to the Station to the weighbridge. They would then come back down into Chapel Lane to go further up to the large gates opening onto the sidings and the cattle pens. Bakers Nursery had a building there for all their deliveries. Items like sugar beet were unloaded and reloaded by hand onto the railway trucks. All down the road, beet lay in gutters having fallen off the lorries. When washed it was quite nice to eat.

A lot of cattle came through the station – mostly for Lee's farm. They would be taken off the trains and walked through the village to the farm on the Wolverhampton Road. The local farmers would bring their milk churns daily to catch the early morning milk train – its guard's van often filled with pigeons being sent all over the country to race. Of course, there were always vans coming from Bakers Nursery full of boxes to be transported all over the country and the world. And many villagers used the train to travel into Wolverhampton, returning to Codsall at the end of the day.

Where the Serendipity shop is now were two wooden shops. Mrs Housden sold general groceries from the one and Mr Alcock ran a butcher's shop in the other. To get to Mrs Housden's you had to walk over a wooden bridge across the stream which ran down the side of the road until it reached the main road when it was piped into the field opposite. Right on the road was a bright and shiny cigarette machine. It dispensed three qualities of cigarettes: Players in a packet of twenty, nicely wrapped in silver paper, Woodbines or for 6d you could have five or ten in a simple open-topped packet. In those days almost everything was fresh, with only a few things sold in tins and packets.

The first thing you would see in Mrs Housden's was a big bag of unwashed potatoes with the top rolled down. Carrots came in bunches with the tops still on and soil on the roots. The same with the beetroot, always in bunches of three. White turnips were very popular. Were they healthier then?

In those days they still used chemical fertilisers and insecticides which are banned today. In those days you bought them as they came out of the ground or out of the clamps where they were protected during the winter. Because they were unwashed, they had a much longer shelf life.

Mrs Housden's grocery shop, next door to Mr Alcock, the butcher.

Mrs Housden also sold tinned goods and there were cakes on the counter. On the left-hand side were the Avery scales. On the floor by the potatoes was the larger pair of scales with a big scoop. On the right side of the counter was a wooden tray about 18 inches square. It was filled with a selection of sweets – liquorice pipes, artificial cigarettes, triangular shapes, sherbet etc.

Everything on the tray was the same price, probably 2d. On the top shelf above the window were the jars of sweets so you could see them from outside. She also sold cigarettes, boxes of matches, general items and candles which were very popular. A lot of things, like biscuits, came in large tins and they stayed in the tins as you made your selection. The range in a small shop was amazing.

Mrs Housden was a very tidy lady with a bunch of keys tied round her waist. She was a good business lady. She had little notebooks and if you wanted to place an order you wrote it down in the book, took it in and when it was ready Mr Housden would put the box on his shoulder and deliver it to you. The Housdens lived in a house on the corner of Chapel Lane and Broadway.

At the back was a lean-to reached from a door behind the counter. One night the lean-to was broken into and all the cigarettes stored in there were taken. The raid was carried out to coincide with a goods train passing so no-one heard the sound of glass breaking.

The window was always decorated for special times of the year: cotton wool to represent snow in winter; fluffy chickens for Easter. Outside was a blind which was pulled down on sunny days. To get to Alcock's butcher's shop next door there was another little wooden bridge to cross. Mr Alcock butchered his own meat. I enjoyed seeing the meat delivered. The van driver would carry half a cow into the shop on his shoulder. The shop was so small that his meat would be hung in the doorway at the front and he would go and fetch his tools to cut up the carcass. There was no refrigerator in the back.

Mr Alcock stands in the doorway of his butcher's shop.

Part of his business was to go round and slaughter people's pigs for them. Mr Alcock lived in a house on the other side of the road. His daughter's husband used to go with him when he went out to kill a pig. At the back of the shops were big tin storage sheds for Codsall Supply Company.

Chapel Lane **(9)** was named after the Free Church Chapel and Hall **(10)**. These buildings occupied the corner plot between Chapel Lane and The Broadway. The Chapel was opened in 1875 and was in use until Trinity Church opened in 1967. It is possible to spot that the houses on this corner are newer than the other houses on either side of them. The chapel and hall were very important in the life of the village.

The former Free Church Chapel and Hall in Chapel Lane.

During and after the War the hall was used as a clinic, where mothers could take their babies to be weighed and pick up their supplies of free orange juice. It was also used to house an overflow class when the school was bursting at the seams and extra accommodation was desperately needed. Miss Farmer was the teacher in charge of these children.

Many of the local children went to Sunday School or the Youth Club because that made them eligible for a day out on a 'charabanc' (coach) to the seaside and a picnic. That was a very rare treat so it was worth spending an hour at Sunday School from

2pm to 3pm in order to be included. The teenagers went to the Youth Club, many for the same reason.

I remember going to the church's annual anniversary event in the Chapel Hall. It was a children's party and I recall someone playing the piano, quite probably it was Mrs Slaney, who only lived two doors away. The youngsters went for the pop and buns which came at the end, but you had to go in your Sunday best with a white shirt, clean shorts and white socks. The church stopped having the celebration when the War started and it never started up again afterwards.

After the gate to the cattle pens there were no houses at all on Chapel Lane until near the top. The houses on the right were built in about 1928. There was a track between them which led into the field at the back. Further up on the railway side lived a man called Fisher who had a wet fish shop at the side of his house.

Chapel Lane before it was widened.

Opposite was a field where he kept the pony, for his pony and trap, which he used when delivering his fish. He stopped when the War started and never restarted afterwards. There were four houses at the top of the lane. Mr Wilkins, a teacher, lived in one and in the others were Mr Alcock, the fuel merchant; another teacher Mrs Westwood and a Miss McGeoch. The top of the lane was so narrow, with high banks, that it was just about wide enough for a car to get through. On the right-hand side was a very deep quarry. There was a sandstone wall, probably blocking the entrance. At the top turning left onto Histons Hill it was all fields. The Rosery, on the other side of the road, was where the Stationmaster lived. At the top of Red Rock Drive was another quarry.

The Farran family:
In the 1940s the Farran family moved from Claregate to a semi-detached Victorian villa on Histons Hill. Proceeding from Chapel Lane it was on the right, approximately 50 yards before the Methodist Church, on the opposite side. A new house called Chestnuts is on the site of the villa.

The Farran family became known because of the war record of their son Roy and the tragic death of Rex, their youngest son. A lane at the side of the villa led to a field extending to Suckling Green Lane. On the morning when the letter bomb was delivered – intended for Roy but mistakenly opened by his brother Rex – I was cycling to school with their younger brother Keith. We saw the postwoman walking along on her way to deliver letters. As soon as we arrived at school, Keith was told to go home.

On the approach to the bridge on the left-hand side were fields. On the right just before the bridge was a footpath which used to lead into another quarry. At the beginning of the War the road for Queens Gardens had just been started but nothing more was done to it until a few years after it ended. From the bridge to the crossroads there were just fields.

Elliotts Lane was quite narrow. The houses at 39-41 were prewar. Further down was a sandstone cottage where Mr Saunders, the furniture maker, lived. His cottage was on a bend and it was pulled down when the road was straightened and widened after the War. On the left-hand side were large houses with extensive front gardens and fields at the back of them.

At the junction with Sandy Lane right on the corner was a smallholding, where Mr Strong kept a few cattle. He had a part-time job as a lamp lighter. He went round on his bike with a long pole which he used to pull the chains which lit the gas lamps. He could do this without getting off his bike.

Proceeding from Elliotts Lane up Sandy Lane, the first smallholding on the right was where Doris and Henry Porteous had a poultry farm and sold fresh eggs. Next to the Porteouses was a similar smallholding which was run as a dairy farm by Mr Jefferies. The dairy herd were Jersey cows producing Grade A milk.

Elliotts Lane where it meets Wolverhampton Road.

Mr Jefferies was always smartly turned out in brown, polished leather gaiters, brown smock and cap. He delivered the milk from shiny metal churns from a superbly turned-out pony and trap. He served the milk in measures. You took your own container and he would give you either a gill (which was ⅛ pint); a ½ pint or 1 pint. The measures had a handle so he could dip it into the churn. Of course it was raw milk straight from the cow.

Later on, Ravenhill Drive was developed the other side of these smallholdings, but before it was built there was nothing until the Barrows Cottages also known as 'the barracks' on the left. These were red brick, low-ceilinged cottages with few amenities.

Further up, a farmer family lived in a long, low, wooden bungalow set back behind a high hedge. As noted earlier, Brabourne

House on the corner with Drury Lane was a goat farm. On the other side of the lane was the white house called Old Drury Cottage. There were so many different small farms around Codsall. I can recall at least sixteen. Many of them were smallholdings given to soldiers after the First World War.

Barrows Cottages with Roseville Gardens being built, 1966.

On the corner where Drury Lane comes out onto Church Road was a Working Men's Club **(29)**. If you turned left you would be returning to the centre of Codsall, over Baker's Way to the Wolverhampton Road. Then past the Nationwide, and we are back to The Bull, The Crown and the centre of Codsall.

We have many publications in print and online available from our website, which also gives details of our monthly meetings and the work of Codsall & Bilbrook History Society.

www.codsallhistory.org

APPENDIX

(1) Site of old cottages, occupied by the Co-op in the 1990s. The end one nearest the Square was a post office.

(2) Site of Codsall Supply Co., corn and seed merchants, which mainly sold animal feedstuffs and supplied local farms and smallholdings.

(3) Codsall House, a late 18th-century Georgian house, extensively renovated after the 1980s. In the first half of the 19th century, it was a ladies' boarding school. More recently it was owned by Major Carr of Wolverhampton Steam Laundry. It was built on the location of the ancient manor house in which lived the Steward of the Manor of Codsall. Fine trees survive in the former grounds of the house.

(4) Parish council offices built on the site of an old barn.

(5) Site of Flemmynge House, a late 19th-century building lived in by the Twentyman and Edge families in the 20th century. After its demolition new houses were built.

(6) Station Road was built about 1844, with walls of sandstone from local quarries (in the 19th century quarrying was a thriving Codsall industry). The original road, prior to the building of the railway station, passed in front of the site of the Old Police House.

(7) The village War Memorial was erected in 1924 and records those killed in the 1914-18 and 1939-45 world wars.

(8) The former Police House was built on land leased in 1880 by the county authorities from two Codsall charities. Its purpose, according to Church records, was for the resident policeman to 'control the turbulent people from Wolverhampton.'

(9) Chapel Lane was once called Pighouse Lane and then Quarry Lane (no doubt because it led from the railway station to the old quarry at the junction between Lansdowne Avenue and Histons Hill).

(10) The site of the Trinity Free Church built in 1873-74 and its Church Hall. The latter was used as a child welfare centre between 1939-45. Both were demolished in 1968.

(11) The village coal merchant was W. Alcock & Son who was located on the station 'wharf' from about 1885 and was a vital business for the village in the days before alternative fuel sources and central heating.

APPENDIX

(12) Codsall Station: the railway was opened on November 12th, 1849, by the Shrewsbury and Birmingham Railway Company which included Shropshire Union Railways and Canal Company and which was amalgamated with the Great Western Railway in 1854. The station became the commercial hub of the village with cattle pens. At its busiest, at least six staff worked at the station. The Rosery in Histons Hill was built for the Stationmaster who, in 1856, was a Mr Evans. The post was held in the Evans family for three generations. The road bridge was built in 1848 and the footbridge in 1888. The bridges and buildings are now protected as Grade II listed by the Department of the Environment (this means that they are protected by law against demolition as structures of regional historic or architectural importance).

(13) The earliest council houses in Codsall. These six pairs were built in about 1919, partly on land owned by the ancient Codsall charities.

(14) Modern shops replaced old shops and cottages. Nearest to The Bull was Codsall Cycle Stores which also sold gramophones and gun cartridges! Bicycles could be stored there whilst their owners went by bus into Wolverhampton. It was run by a Mrs Hancock. At the lower end, the Bird sisters had a sweet shop.

(15) Sawpit Lane, or Claypit Lane, gave access to Wolverhampton Road to Station Road.

(16) The Bull. At some time before 1783 it was called The Tiled House but the actual date of the original building is not known.

(17) The site of The Mount, a substantial house built in 1840 for Thomas Harley, a wine merchant in Wolverhampton. It was demolished in the 1960s and replaced by smaller houses.

(18) The corner shop in the 1920s was A.L. Harvey Central Stores and Post Office. The stores probably opened in the early 1900s, in premises built after 1850.

(19) The timber-framed building was one of five houses on this site in 1850 and is reputedly one of the oldest dwellings in Codsall. It might have provided lodgings for Cromwell's soldiers in 1651 (see History Society publication Mrs Cockerill's Memories). In recent years it has been an Indian Restaurant.

(20) The building that stood here was the HQ of the Home Guard during

APPENDIX

the 1939-45 War and had a siren at roof level. It was probably the original Primitive Methodist Chapel which was built about 1825.

(21) An old brick building (which is still there) alongside Mount Cottage was the location used by the Local Defence Volunteers, as the Home Guard was originally known. They wore white armbands bearing the letters LDV.

(22) A timber building probably dating from the 1914-18 War was sited here. It was Blanton's Tea Room and became the Forget-Me-Not Club after the tea room burnt down in 1968.

(23) The site of Roseville Farm. A dairy farm which was demolished when the bypass was built. Housing development started on the farmland in the 1960s.

(24) Vaughan Cottages, retained as part of the new housing development, had access from a track on the east side of Roseville Farm. The gardens, containing fruit trees, ran up to the line of the present footpath from Wolverhampton Road to Drury Lane.

(25) Site of Georgian-style cottages dating from 1724 which contained the Cottage Press until demolished for the bypass.

(26) Site of a smithy, blacksmith and wheelwright later a garage and subsequently a retail shop. 'Lucky' Law made coffins here in the 1920s.

(27) This was the location of Warner's Field which was used for village events and where grew several Tettenhall Dick pear trees. In the 1930s, Captain Cecil Warner lived opposite in a Georgian-style Old House which has now been demolished.

(28) Church Road, cobbled in years gone by, was known as Church Street and shown as such on Ordnance Survey maps until about 1930.

(29) A Working Men's Club in a wooden building stood on this corner site in the 1930s. It was preceded by cottages which fronted onto Church Street.

(30) Location of the Co-operative Stores in the first half of the 20th century.

(31) Brabourne: a 19th-century house which had been used as a goat farm.

(32) The Old Cottage was a bakery at one time and the building is believed to date from 1574.

(33) Cherry Tree Cottage was at one time two cottages.

(34) The new National School, opened in 1864 prior to the Education Act of 1870. In 1906 it became the Codsall Church of England School. In 1976 it became a First School occupying both the existing site and a new site east of Drury Lane, which had been opened in 1965. Finally the school moved out of the 1864 buildings into the new premises.

(35) The Mill House includes a tower mill. It was in use until just over a century ago. In earlier centuries there were two water mills and a horse mill in the area around Codsall.

(36) It is fairly certain that the village pound was sited in the immediate vicinity of the Church.

(37) The Parish Church of St Nicholas, parts of which date from the 12th century, with its Norman Doorway and 14th-century tower. The Church was substantially rebuilt and extended in 1849 and restored in 1958. The Wrottesley tomb is located in the chancel.

(38) The Victorian Vicarage was built in about 1849 and owned in 1850 by Lord Wrottesley with the Revd A. Trower as tenant. The site was formerly occupied by the Holly Bush public house.

(39) The Tithe Map of 1849 indicates the small site (about 100 square yards) occupied by the original National School, built in 1818 and owned in 1850 by the Church Overseers. Just behind the school was John Fletcher's house and blacksmith's shop (with access from Mill Lane, now called Church Lane). John Fletcher died in 1881 and is buried in the churchyard.

(40) Manor Court (Clifton House) is a late 19th-century house on land which was included in the 1849 Tithe Map as a croft.

(41) The Parish Rooms were built in 1907 as a Parish Institute. On the north side and sharing a footpath access off Church Street was a cobbler's shop. The cobbler, earlier in the 20th century, was Will Jones the brother-in-law of Mrs Cockerill. He lived next door in premises which became the offices of the Registrar of Births, Marriages and Deaths and subsequently part of a renovated group of buildings.

(42) The Cottage is the birthplace of sculptor Sir Charles Wheeler, past President of the Royal Academy. The modest grave of Sir Charles and Lady Wheeler is in the churchyard east of the Church. On the side of the house a small annexe was used as a post office by Joseph Fletcher and his wife.

(43) Russell House and the location of Bakers' Nurseries. Before 1900 it was Old Hall Farm, the fields of which extended to the west and north-west. After 1903 it was developed by the Baker family into a firm of international repute which became the major employer in the village. In the late 1930s, George Russell was brought to the firm from Yorkshire and achieved wide recognition for the development of the Russell Lupin. Also developed here were the Bishop Delphinium and the Symon-Jeune Phlox.

(44) Statue of the Lone Singer, bequeathed to the village by sculptor, Sir Charles Wheeler. It was placed in position after his death in 1976. He had originally intended to produce a special sculpture for the village instead of the Lone Singer.

(45) The Crown is an 18th-century building with several additions and alterations (look at the elevation to Wood Road) and included stables and outbuildings to serve its early role as a coaching inn.

(46) The Firs was a farmhouse and also, during the 1939-45 War, a factory. It subsequently became the local headquarters of the Conservative Party and housed the offices of the (Conservative) MP for South Staffordshire.

(47) Spencer's butcher's shop, which had its own slaughterhouse attached for several years after the War. It remained a butcher's shop, run by Andrew MacLeod, until fairly recently and is believed to be the only shop in the village which had continued in the same use for several generations. Its telephone number used to be 11.

(48) York's (also known as Stockton's) Grocery and Provision Store was in the corner building. It was the original village store dating from the 18th century.

www.ingramcontent.com/pod-product-compliance
Lightning Source LLC
Chambersburg PA
CBHW061306040426
42444CB00010B/2541